OUR SOLAR SYSTEM

Constellations

BY DANA MEACHEN RAU

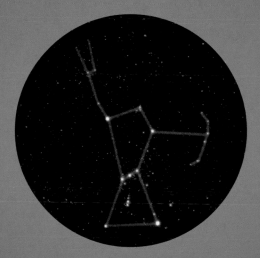

Content Adviser: Dr. Stanley P. Jones, Assistant Director, Washington, D.C., Operations, NASA-Sponsored Classroom of the Future

Science Adviser: Terrence E. Young Jr., M.Ed., M.L.S., Jefferson Parish (Louisiana) Public School System

Reading Adviser: Susan Kesselring, M.A., Literacy Educator, Rosemount-Apple Valley-Eagan (Minnesota) School District

COMPASS POINT BOOKS

MINNEAPOLIS, MINNESOTA

For my friends at the Farmington Library—D.M.R.

Compass Point Books
3109 West 50th Street, #115
Minneapolis, MN 55410

Visit Compass Point Books on the Internet at *www.compasspointbooks.com*
or e-mail your request to *custserv@compasspointbooks.com*

Photographs ©: Roger Ressmeyer/Corbis, cover, 1, 13, 21; Bettmann/Corbis, 3, 9, 11, 17; Richard Hamilton Smith/DPA Photo, 4–5; Mary Evans Picture Library, 5 (right), 19; NASA, 6 (bottom); Werner Forman/Art Resource, N.Y., 7; Hulton/Archive by Getty Images, 8; Astronomical Society of the Pacific, 15, 20, 22; Denis Scott/Corbis, 18; Stapleton Collection/Corbis, 23; DigitalVision, 25; Vince Varnas, 26; Ken Wardius/Index Stock Imagery, 27 (top); Daniel Hodges, 27 (bottom); Kym Thalassoudis, 28, 29.

Editor: Nadia Higgins
Lead Designer/Page production: The Design Lab
Photo researcher: Svetlana Zhurkina
Educational Consultant: Diane Smolinski

Managing Editor: Catherine Neitge
Art Director: Keith Griffin
Production Director: Keith McCormick
Creative Director: Terri Foley

Library of Congress Cataloging-in-Publication Data
 Rau, Dana Meachen, 1971–
 Constellations / By Dana Meachen Rau.
    p. cm. — (Our solar system)
 Includes index.
 ISBN 0-7565-0850-9 (hardcover)
 1. Constellations—Juvenile literature. I. Title.
 QB802.R28 2005
 523.8—dc22   2004015568

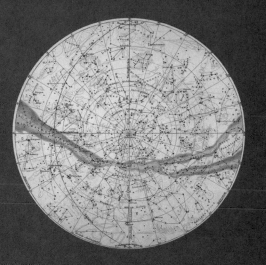

Table of Contents

Star Gazing

Have you ever been on a camping trip? You might sit around a fire, roast marsh-mallows, and tell stories. You might gaze up at the night sky. The farther you are from city lights, the more stars you can see. On a clear, dark night, you can see thousands of stars.

The stars in the sky might just look like a jumble of dots. It may be hard to find the same star twice. Try connecting the dots, as if the sky were a dot-to-dot game. Imagine pictures made up of the dots you connect. You will find it easier to spot a certain star again if you imagine it as part of a picture.

This is what early sky watchers did. They noticed that some groups of stars seemed to form pictures.

◀ *Away from city lights, the night sky is filled with starlight.*

▼ *The ancient Greek astronomer Hipparchus looked for constellations in the night sky.*

They noticed these pictures seemed to move across the sky each evening. They could look at a certain star and find it again the next night by looking for the same pattern of stars they had seen the night before. The sky watchers called these patterns of stars constellations, which means "stars together" in Latin. They gave the constellations names, such as the Southern Cross and the Goldfish, that described the patterns the stars formed.

The Southern Cross constellation ▲

From Earth, the stars in a constellation look like they are the same distance away. Yet in reality, some stars in a constellation are much closer to Earth than others.

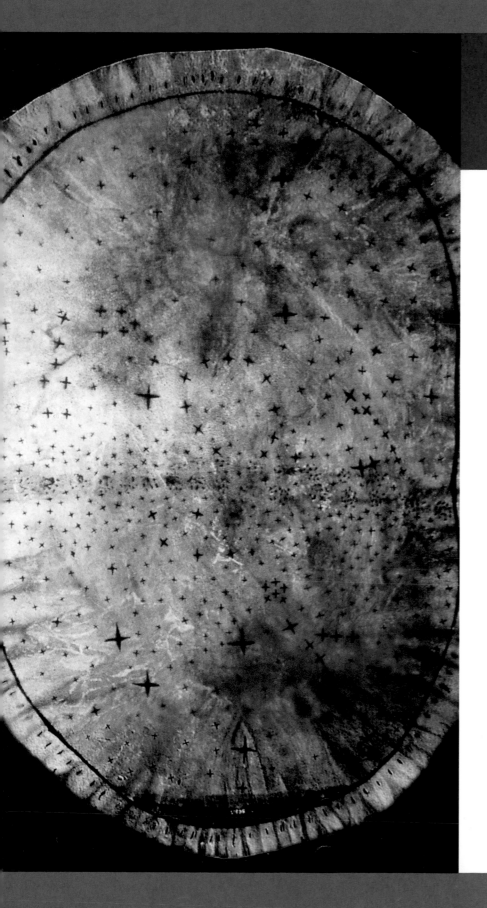

Ancient people noticed patterns in the stars. How do we know this? Scientists have found writings and drawings on old coins and pottery. Some of these earliest records are 6,000 years old. They were found in the area that we call the Middle East today. Other ancient drawings of star patterns have been found in China, Egypt, and the Americas.

The ancient Greeks were fascinated by the night sky. Nearly 2,000 years ago,

◀ *Ancient Pawnee Indians made this chart of the night sky out of leather.*

Ptolemy (pronounced TAHL-uh-mee) wrote descriptions of 48 constellations. Today, we know of even more constellations. Ptolemy knew of only 48 because he had not traveled far from his home in Alexandria, Egypt. He had only seen the night sky in and near his own city. He could not see parts of the sky that other people could see from their cities in other countries.

In the 1500s, adventurers started exploring the rest of the world. As they traveled, they noticed the night sky looked different than it

In 150 A.D., Ptolemy wrote a book called the Almagest in which he described 48 constellations. ▶

did above their own lands and seas. They saw many stars and star patterns that they had never seen before. They drew maps of the sky and created new constellations.

From the 1500s to the 1700s, many new constellations were added to the list. Today, the final number of constellations is 88. All of the stars that you can see without a telescope are part of a constellation.

▼ *An astronomer from the Middle Ages, about 800 years ago, takes measurements of the night sky.*

The Changing Sky

You can't see all 88 constellations at the same time because Earth is round like a ball. Your view of the sky is different, depending on where you are.

The Earth is divided into halves, called hemispheres. The Northern Hemisphere is the top half of Earth, and the Southern Hemisphere is the bottom half. There are some constellations that only people in the Northern Hemisphere can see, and some that can be seen only in the south.

During an evening, constellations seem to travel across the sky, but the stars are not moving at all—Earth is! Earth spins around on its axis the way a top spins on its tip. Earth, however, makes only one complete turn every day. This is what makes the stars seem to pass through the sky each night. This is also what causes the stars to rise and

This historical map of the sky shows the constellations visible only in the Northern Hemisphere. ▶

The equator is an imaginary line that runs around the middle of Earth. People who live at the equator can see all 88 constellations during the course of the year.

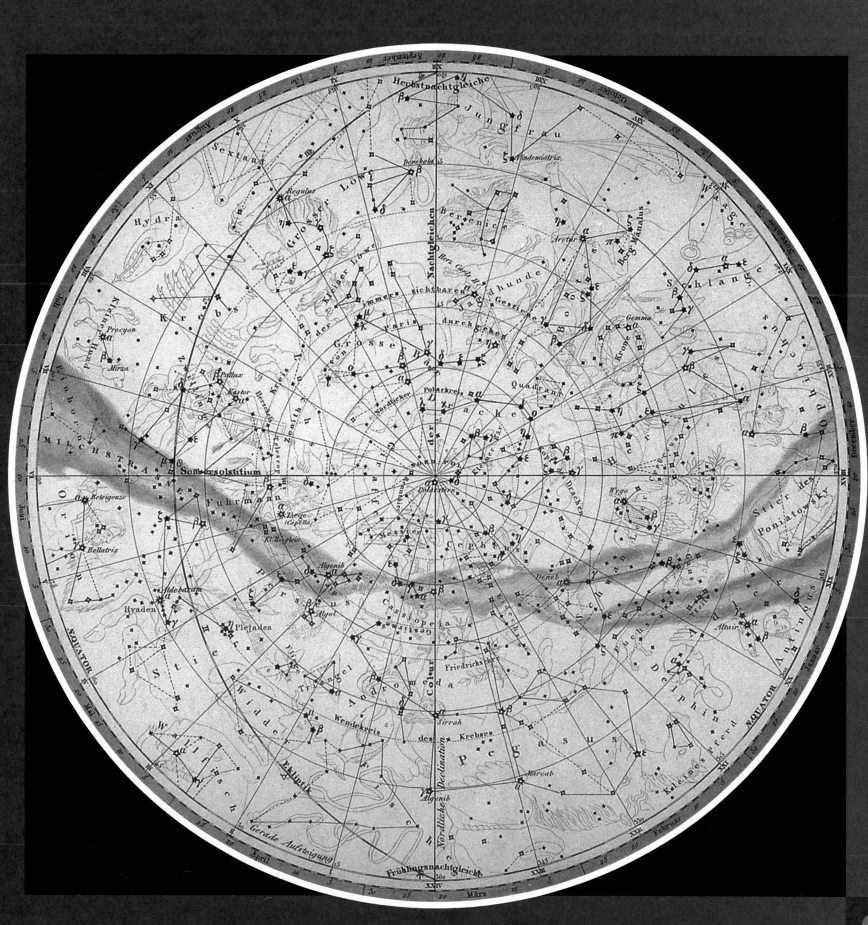

set as they come in and out of our view.

As it spins, Earth travels, or revolves, around the sun in a path called an orbit. It takes one year for Earth to orbit the sun. As it travels, Earth tilts either toward the sun or away from it, which causes the seasons to change. During each season, Earth is in a different location in its orbit. That means the constellations we see from Earth change with the seasons. You may not be able to see the same constellations in the summer that you see in the winter.

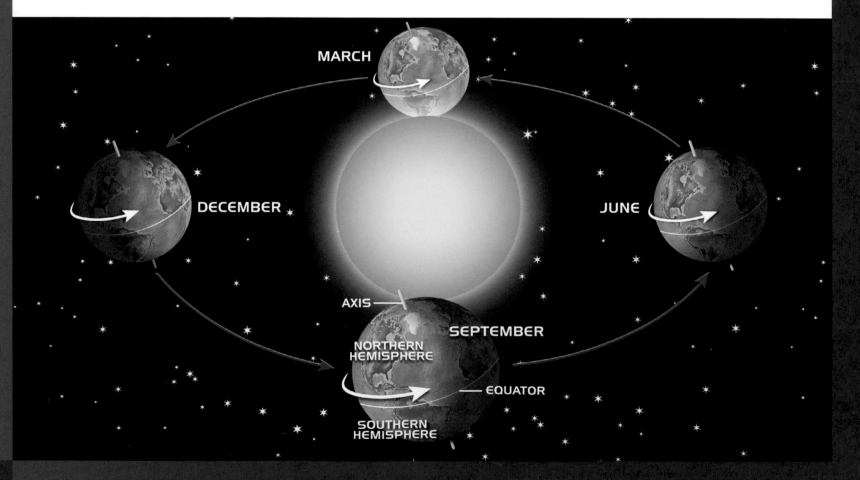

MARCH

DECEMBER

JUNE

AXIS

SEPTEMBER

NORTHERN HEMISPHERE

EQUATOR

SOUTHERN HEMISPHERE

Types of Constellations

There are three types of constellations: circumpolar constellations, seasonal constellations, and zodiac constellations.

Circumpolar means "around the pole." Circumpolar constellations appear in the areas above Earth's North Pole and South Pole. If the sky is clear, you can always see these constellations, no matter what time of night it is. These constellations never rise or set in the sky, and they move very little. Polaris, or the North Star, never seems to move at all. It is directly above the North Pole. The northern

▼ *The arrow shows Polaris, or the North Star, above an observatory. The lines circling Polaris are other stars that appear as lines in this photograph.*

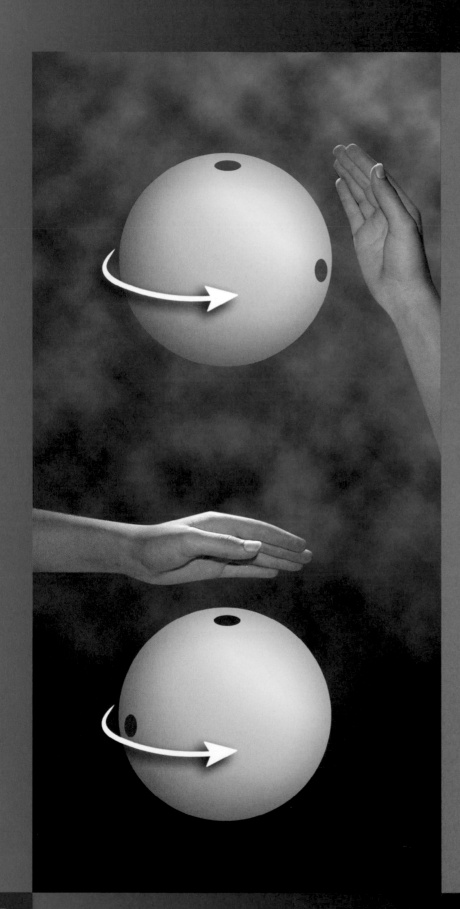

Why don't circumpolar constellations rise and set like other stars? The answer has to do with two facts—first, that Earth is rotating, and second, that these stars are by Earth's poles. Imagine you have a spinning ball with a red mark on its side and a blue one on top. Now imagine your hand is a star. When you put your hand by the ball's side, it faces the red marker only half of the time. If you put your hand directly above the ball, it faces the blue marker the whole time. Like a circumpolar constellation, your hand stays in view of the blue marker as the ball spins.

circumpolar constellations circle Polaris.

Seasonal constellations are ones that are visible during a certain season. In the winter, Orion (the Hunter) is a constellation you would be sure to notice if you lived in the Northern Hemisphere. The three stars of Orion's belt are hard to miss. Hercules is a very large constellation visible in summer in the north. A square of stars makes up his body, and lines of stars seem to complete the picture with arms and legs.

Zodiac constellations are ones you would see if you were trying to find the planets

◀ *The constellation Hercules is visible only during summer.*

(except Pluto) through a telescope. To viewers on Earth, these 12 constellations seem to form a path through which the sun and planets travel during the course of the year. The sun moves through about one zodiac constellation each month. During the day, it's too bright for us to see the sun's path, but the stars are still there.

This sky chart from the 1600s shows the ▶
zodiac constellations as 12 symbols
(in the outer ring).

The 12 Zodiac Constellations
The word *zodiac* means "circle of living things."

Latin Name	Common Name
Leo	.The Lion
Cancer	.The Crab
Gemini (*JEM-in-eye*)	.The Twins
Taurus (*TORE-us*)	.The Bull
Aries (*AIR-eez*)	.The Ram
Pisces (*PIE-seez*)	.The Fishes
Aquarius (*uh-KWAIR-ee-us*)	.The Water Carrier (a man holding a jug of water)
Capricornus (*CAP-rih-corn-us*)	.The Sea Goat
Sagittarius (*saa-jih-TARE-ee-us*)	.The Archer (a man with a bow and arrow)
Scorpius (*SCORE-pee-us*)	.The Scorpion
Libra (*LEE-bra*)	.The Scales (weighing scales)
Virgo (*VER-go*)	.The Virgin (a woman with wings)

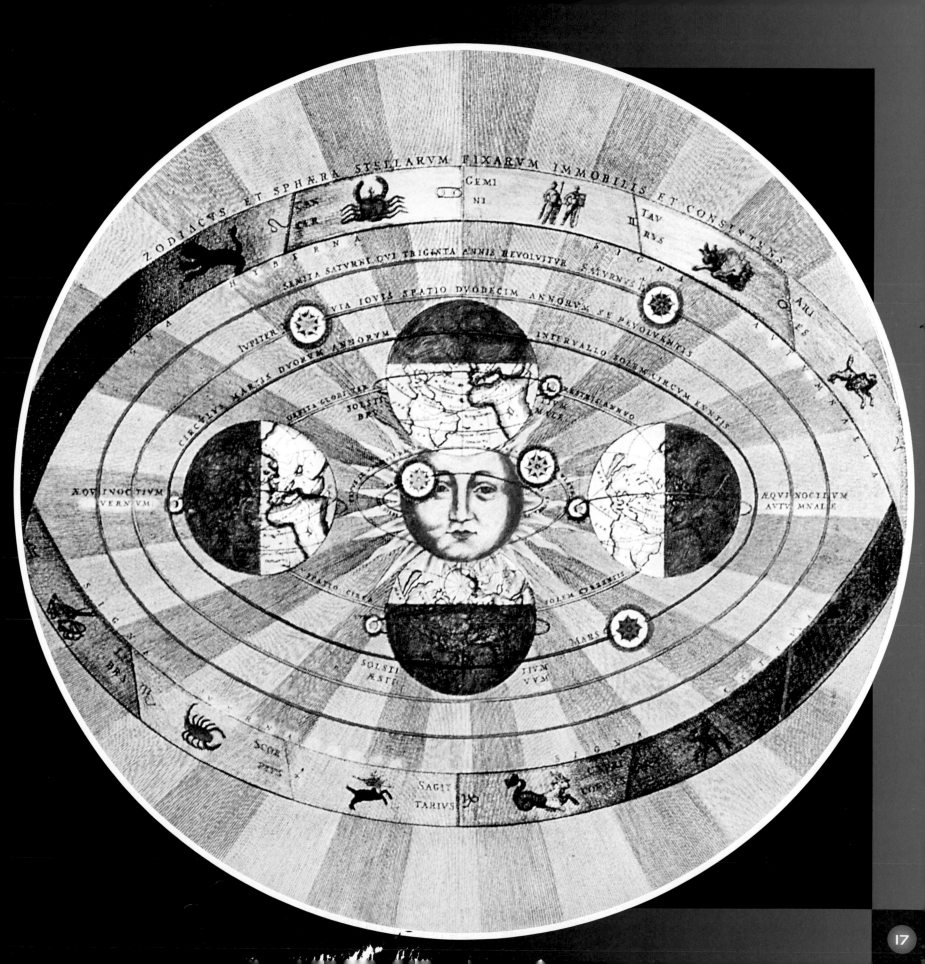

Naming
the Stars

You may notice that not all constellations look like their names. Taurus the Bull, for example, does not really look like a bull. It just looks like two lines of stars. Early sky watchers used their imaginations to fill in the rest of the picture.

The ancient Greeks named many of the constellations after the gods and goddesses of their religion as well as after heroes such as Perseus (pronounced PURSE-ee-us) and his love

This illustration of Taurus shows how ▼ viewers must use their imaginations to see the pictures constellations make.

Andromeda (pronounced an-DROHM-ih-duh). We call the stories about these gods and heroes myths. The characters in Greek myths led very exciting lives.

The Greeks also named constellations after animals, such as Pisces (the Fish) and Aquila (the Eagle). They named constellations after imaginary animals, too, such as Pegasus, a horse with wings.

Hundreds of years later, sky watchers in the Southern

▲ *Ancient Greeks named a constellation after Perseus, a hero from Greek myth.*

Hemisphere used some new ideas to name the southern constellations. Many are named after scientific tools the sky watchers used in their work, such as the Telescope and the Microscope constellations. People also named them after everyday objects, such as the constellation Horologium (pronounced hor-uh-LOW-jee-um), which means clock. They named constellations after animals, too, but often after more unusual creatures, such as a chameleon or toucan.

The constellation Pegasus was named ▶ after an imaginary horse with wings.

Stories in the Stars

Ancient people created stories about the animals and people they saw in the stars. Constellation stories come from all parts of the world, including Greece, China, Egypt, South America, North America, and the Middle East. Two constellations, Ursa Major (the Great Bear) and Orion (the Hunter), are favorite subjects of these ancient stories.

The Big Dipper is one of the easiest patterns of stars to spot. It is made up of seven very bright stars. The Big Dipper is not its own constellation but is actually part of Ursa Major.

▼ *The Big Dipper looks like a ladle with a long handle.*

The Navajo Indians of North America told a story about the seven bright stars of the Big Dipper. In the story, a woman marries a bear. When her father kills it, she turns into a bear herself, and tries to kill her younger sister and seven brothers. The seven brothers escape to the sky and become the stars.

In a Hindu story, the seven stars are seven wise men, called *Rishis,* who were in charge of the rising of the sun. The Greeks believed Ursa Major was Callisto, a goddess who had been changed into a bear and was

The three stars of Orion's belt make this ▸
constellation easy to recognize.

almost killed by her son, Arcas, by mistake.

Orion is a hunter from a Greek myth. Three bright stars make up his belt and other stars represent his shoulders, club, and shield. Two nearby constellations, Canis Major (the Big Dog) and Canis Minor (the Little Dog) are his pets.

In one story, Orion is swimming in the sea. Nearby, the goddess Artemis is showing off her hunting skills, and she kills Orion by mistake. She is so sad that she puts his body in the sky.

In another story, Orion brags to everyone that he is so strong that no animal could ever kill him. When he comes across a tiny scorpion, he kills it, but not before it stings him first. Orion dies soon after. That is why the constellation Scorpius (the Scorpion) and Orion are very far apart. When one rises, the other sets. They are never in the sky together.

▲ *This is how one artist has imagined Orion in the night sky.*

How We Use Constellations

*★ Today, astronomers use constellations as a map of the sky. In 1928, the International Astronomical Union designed the map by dividing the sky into 88 areas around each constellation.

The word *constellation* does not just mean a pattern of stars. It also refers to the area of the sky that surrounds the constellation. For example, a star in Scorpius might not be one that makes the picture of the scorpion. That star might be a fainter star that is in the same area of the sky as the scorpion picture.

Long ago, farmers used the constellations like a calendar. In some places of the world, the weather did not change enough for farmers to know what time of year it was. When a certain constellation was visible in the sky, they knew it was spring and time to plant certain crops. Then, when another constellation rose, they knew winter was coming, and it was time to gather their crops.

Constellations also helped people in their travels. Explorers of new lands often traveled by ship. At sea, the explorers did not have landmarks, such as mountains or rivers, to guide them. Instead, they used the stars to navigate. By knowing the circumpolar constellations, they could figure out which direction was north or south.

They could navigate their ships to the land they wished to find. Even today, navigators in spacecraft use the stars to guide them.

▼ *The* Pioneer *spacecraft has star sensors that help it navigate through outer space.*

Constellations connect us with the past. When you look up at the sky today, you are looking at the same sky people have studied for thousands of years. The sky is filled with pictures. The people who created them had many stories to tell. We can use our own imaginations to make up new stories as we gaze into the sky.

Orion (left) and Taurus ▶
are partly visible here.

PLANISPHERE

Look through the window to see the main stars visible in the heavens for every night of the year.

Latitude 42° North
U.S.A. - Southern Europe - Northern Japan

A star chart is a helpful tool in finding constellations at certain times of the year. The chart is circle-shaped and marked with months along its edges. An oval-shaped window shows the stars that are visible at certain times of the year, with the constellations connected by lines.

Chart of Constellations
Northern Hemisphere

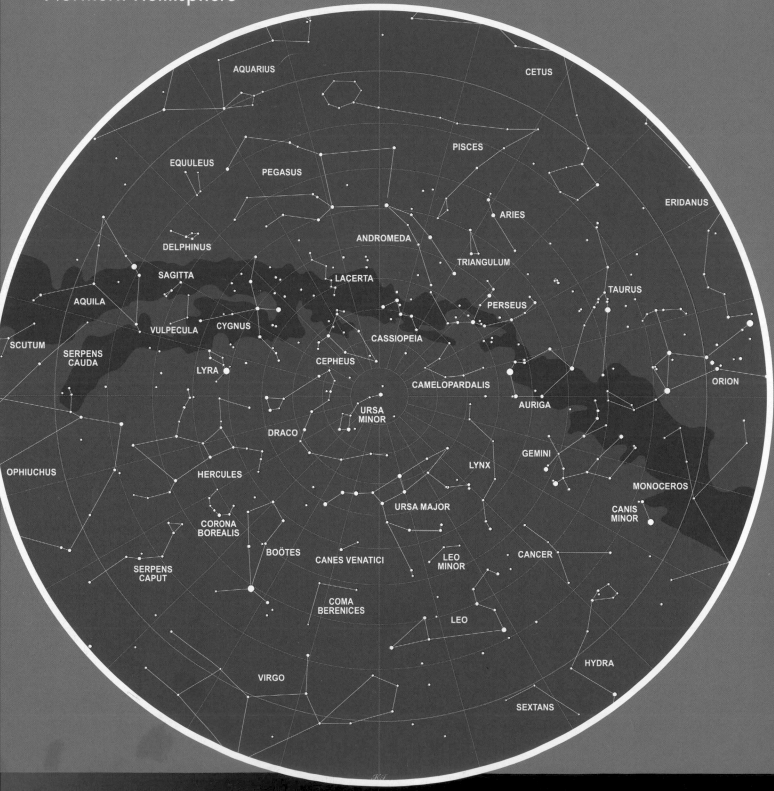

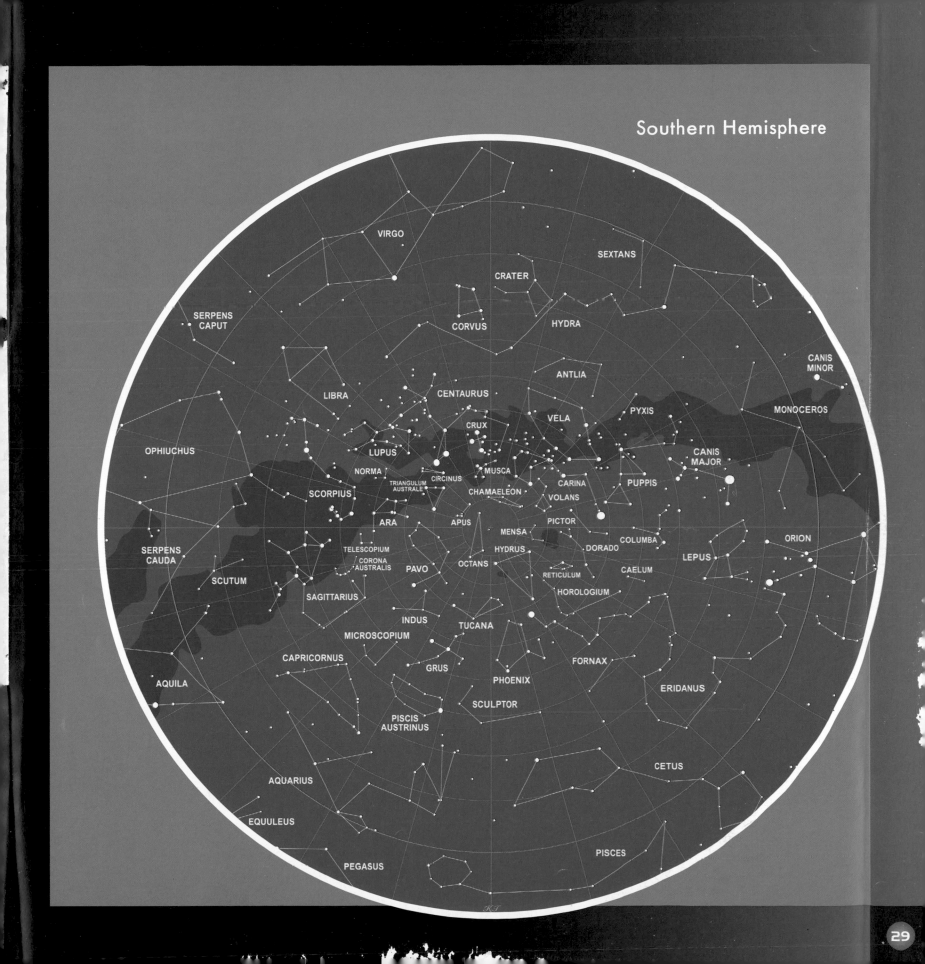

Southern Hemisphere

29

Glossary

axis—an imaginary line running through the center of Earth from the North Pole to the South Pole

International Astronomical Union—a group of astronomers in charge of naming objects in space

Latin—an ancient language that was spoken in western Europe

Middle East—a region of the world that covers Arabic-speaking countries and a few others around northern Africa and southwestern Asia

mythology—ancient stories, usually about gods and goddesses

navigate—to find one's way while traveling

Did You Know?

- The easiest way to find the North Star is to find the Big Dipper. First, find the two stars at the end of the Dipper's "bowl." A line up from them will lead you right to Polaris.

- In 275 B.C., the ancient Greek Aratus of Soli (ca. 315–245 B.C.) wrote a poem called "Phaenomena," which contains the earliest known list of constellations.

- Throughout history and even today, some people think the stars can control the actions of people on Earth. They use the constellations of the zodiac in an attempt to predict the future.

- Each star in the sky has a name. Many of them still have Arabic names from ancient times. Others are named based on which constellation they are in. For example, the star Altair is also known as Alpha Aquilae. *Alpha* means "brightest," and *Aquilae* means "the constellation of Aquila." So the star's name means "the brightest star in Aquila."

- Betelgeuse (pronounced beetle-juice) is the brightest star in the constellation Orion. People say that its name, which may come from Arabic, means "the armpit of the giant."

Want to Know More?

AT THE LIBRARY

Ford, Harry. *The Young Astronomer.* New York: Dorling Kindersley, 1998.

Gifford, Clive. *The Kingfisher Facts and Records Book of Space.* New York: Kingfisher, 2001.

Mitton, Jacqueline. *A Zoo in the Sky: A Book of Animal Constellations.* Washington, D.C.: National Geographic Society, 1998.

Vogt, Gregory L. *Constellations.* Mankato, Minn.: Bridgestone Books, 2003.

ON THE WEB

For more information on **constellations,** use FactHound to track down Web sites related to this book.

1. Go to *www.facthound.com*
2. Type in a search word related to this book or this book ID: **0756508509**.
3. Click on the *Fetch It* button.

Your trusty FactHound will fetch the best Web sites for you!

ON THE ROAD

Adler Planetarium and Astronomy Museum
1300 S. Lake Shore Drive
Chicago, IL 60605-2403
312/922-STAR
To visit the oldest planetarium in the Western Hemisphere

National Air and Space Museum
Sixth and Independence Avenue Southwest
Washington, DC 20560
202/357-2700
To learn more about the solar system and space exploration

National Radio Astronomy Observatory
The Very Large Array
P.O. Box O
1003 Lopezville Road
Socorro, NM 87801-0387
505/835-7000
To see a collection of 27 radio antennae that are always collecting the energy coming from deep space

Mount Wilson Observatory
Mount Wilson, CA 91023
626/793-3100
To see the telescope that many famous astronomers have used to study the night sky

Index

◄ **About the Author:** *Dana Meachen Rau loves to study space. Her office walls are covered with pictures of planets, astronauts, and spacecraft. She also likes to look up at the sky with her telescope and write poems about what she sees. Ms. Rau is the author of more than 100 books for children, including nonfiction, biographies, storybooks, and early readers. She lives in Burlington, Connecticut, with her husband, Chris, and children, Charlie and Allison.*